WALT DISNEY PICTURES'
Return To
OZ

SCHOLASTIC INC.
New York Toronto London Auckland Sydney

ISBN: 0-590-33747-5

12 11 10 9 8 7 6 5 4 3 2 1   7   5 6 7 8 9/8 0/9
Printed in the U.S.A.

IT'S AFTER ONE, AND SHE'S STILL NOT ASLEEP! SHE KEEPS TALKING ABOUT A PLACE THAT DOES NOT EXIST— SAYS SHE'S BEEN THERE!

"SHE CALLS IT 'OZ,' THE 'EMERALD CITY.'

EMERALD CITY— HA! WHO EVER HEARD OF SUCH A PLACE?"

"AND SHE TALKS ABOUT A 'TIN MAN,' AND A 'COWARDLY LION,' AND ABOUT A SCARECROW WHO'S A KING..."

OH, HENRY! I'M SO WORRIED ABOUT HER! SHE DOESN'T SEEM TO KNOW THE DIFFERENCE BETWEEN IMAGINATION AND REALITY!

NOW, EM...

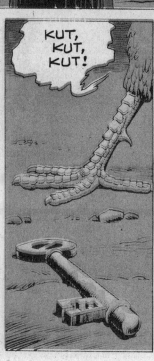

I HOPE DOCTOR WORLEY'S TREATMENT DOESN'T TAKE LONG! IT'LL BE LONELY HERE WITHOUT DOROTHY!

IT SURE WILL BE, EM!

UNCLE HENRY! AUNT EM!

I FOUND IT!! BILLINA HAD IT IN HER BEAK!

YOU FOUND WHAT?

THIS KEY! IT'S FROM OZ! IT'S PROOF THAT I DIDN'T DREAM IT! OZ DOES EXIST!

NOW, DOROTHY—THIS IS JUST THE KEY TO OUR OLD HOUSE! YOU REMEMBER—THE ONE THAT THE TORNADO DESTROYED!

I DO REMEMBER, BUT THIS CAN'T BE THE KEY TO OUR OLD HOUSE! IT'S FROM OZ!

THE SCARECROW SENT IT! I KNOW HE NEEDS MY HELP!

NOW, DOROTHY...

NEXT WEEK I'LL TAKE YOU TO A CLINIC, DOROTHY! THEY'LL HELP YOU FORGET THIS OZ NONSENSE!

AND SO, A WEEK LATER, DOROTHY AND AUNT EM ARE ON THEIR WAY TO DOCTOR WORLEY'S CLINIC...

AUNT EM, WHY CAN'T I TAKE TOTO WITH ME?

DOCTOR WORLEY'S TREATMENT MAY TAKE SEVERAL DAYS! THEY HAVE NO PLACE FOR TOTO TO STAY!

DON'T WORRY, MRS. BLUE! AFTER THE TREATMENT, DOROTHY WILL BE FINE!

THEN CAN I GO BACK TO OZ?

YOU WON'T NEED THOSE DREAMS ANYMORE, DOROTHY!

THIS MACHINE WILL HELP YOU SLEEP AGAIN!

THAT LOOKS LIKE A FACE, DOESN'T IT?

THE BRAIN IS MERELY AN ELECTRICAL, MACHINE, MADAME! BAD DREAMS ARE SIMPLY MAL-FUNCTIONS!

HM...

YOUR NIECE IS IN GOOD HANDS, MRS. BLUE! IN A WEEK'S TIME, SHE WILL BE AS GOOD AS NEW!

A WEEK?! BUT, AUNT EM...

BE A GOOD GIRL, DOROTHY!

DO WHATEVER DR. WORLEY AND NURSE WILSON TELL YOU! I'LL BE BACK SOON!

E-EEE-E-EEEE-EE

THAT'S FUNNY— I THOUGHT I HEARD SOMEONE MOAN . . . OR DID I?

HERE WE ARE, DOROTHY!

WILSON, GET EVERYTHING READY! I'LL BE BACK SOON!

I MUST SEE TO THAT, ER . . . NOISE!

WH-WHERE ARE WE GOING?

SILENCE! FROM NOW ON, YOU WILL SPEAK ONLY WHEN YOU'RE SPOKEN TO!

THIS IS THE NEW PATIENT! PREPARE HER!

BUT . . .

WHY DO YOU HAVE TO TIE ME DOWN?

MERELY TO KEEP YOU FROM FALLING OFF THE TABLE!

!

HMMM... THAT'S QUITE A STORM!

NO MATTER—IT SHOULDN'T AFFECT THE TREATMENT!

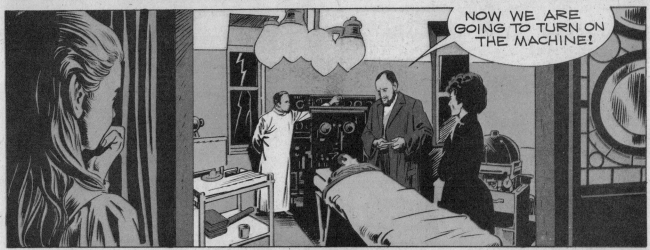

NOW WE ARE GOING TO TURN ON THE MACHINE!

YOU MUST WEAR THESE, DOROTHY!

CRASH

NOW, MY DEAR, HOLD STILL...

SHE'S SEEN US! **RUN! RUN!**

WHERE DO YOU THINK YOU'RE GOING?

NURSE WILSON AND DR. WORLEY ARE AWFUL PEOPLE!

THEIR ELECTRICAL "TREATMENTS" HAVE HURT PEOPLE!

COME BACK HERE, YOU LITTLE BRATS!

THE RIVER! IT'S OUR ONLY CHANCE!

BUT...

WE'RE GOING TO DROWN!

GRAB ONTO THAT CHICKEN COOP, DOROTHY!

"DON'T WORRY ABOUT ME"...

THE NEXT MORNING...

I MUST HAVE FALLEN ASLEEP! BUT WHERE'S MY FRIEND?

SHE HELPED ME GET AWAY... BUT NOW I'M ALONE...

ALONE?! THE VERY IDEA! WHAT DO YOU MEAN, "ALONE"?

BEYOND THE DEADLY DESERT...

KUT-KUT-KUT! I'M STILL HUNGRY, DOROTHY!

SO AM I, BILLINA!

IF I CAN FIND A LUNCHPAIL TREE, WE CAN EAT!

THANK GOODNESS! ONCE WE HAVE EATEN, WE CAN GO ON TO EMERALD CITY AND SEE THE SCARECROW!

THE FACT THAT WE'RE HERE MUST MEAN HE NEEDS HELP!

KUT-KUT!

WHAT IS IT, BILLINA?

"BEWARE THE WHEELERS"... WHAT ON EARTH ARE "WHEELERS"?

OH, WELL— IT CAN'T BE IMPORTANT! LET'S EAT, BILLINA! I'M STARVING!

THE WONDERFUL AIR IN OZ GIVES ME A BIG APPETITE!

OINK! OINK!

BILLINA! GOOD HEAVENS! LOOK!

HEE, HEE, HEE, HEE...

WHAT IN THE WORLD IS THAT?!

OINK! OINK! OINK!

HEE HEE

THEY DON'T LOOK FRIENDLY! RUN, BILLINA!

A CHICKEN! HERE, CHICK, CHICK, CHICK! COME ON, CHICKEN!

IS HE TALKING TO YOU OR TO ME?

I DON'T KNOW, BILLINA!

BUT WE'RE NOT STAYING AROUND TO FIND OUT!

OH, NO! A DOOR! AND IT'S LOCKED!

GOT YOU NOW, CHICKEN, CHICKEN! YOU'RE TRAPPED!

KUT! WE NEED A KEY!

A KEY... MAYBE I CAN USE THAT ONE YOU FOUND!

YOU KNOW, BILLINA — THE ONE THAT SAID "OZ"!

CLICK!

I WAS RIGHT! IT'S OPENING!

THOUGH, I MUST SAY, IT DOESN'T LOOK MUCH SAFER IN HERE!

ROBBERS! LUNCHPAIL THIEVES! COME OUT OF THERE!

YOU TOOK A MEAL FROM THE LUNCHPAIL TREE WITHOUT THE NOME KING'S PERMISSION!

I NEVER HEARD OF ANY **NOME** KING! THE SCARECROW IS THE KING OF OZ!

KUT-KUT KUT!

DOROTHY! LOOK!

IT'S A BIG COPPER EGG—BUT I'VE NEVER SEEN AN EGG WITH LEGS...

IT LOOKS LIKE A MECHANICAL MAN!

KUT-KUT! IMAGINE THAT—AN EGG-SHAPED MAN!

KUT-KUT! LOOK—A SIGN! READ IT, DOROTHY!

"PATENTED CLOCKWORK MECHANICAL MAN. WIND HIM UP TO THINK, WORK AND SPEAK! GUARANTEED FOR 1,000 YEARS."

OH, DOROTHY—YOU DON'T BELIEVE EVERYTHING YOU READ, DO YOU?

I DON'T KNOW!

I'LL WIND HIM UP! NOW WE'LL SEE!

THERE!

THANK-YOU FOR WINDING ME UP, MISS GALE! ALLOW ME TO INTRODUCE MYSELF!

WAIT A MINUTE! HOW DO YOU KNOW MY NAME?

I AM TIK TOK, THE ROYAL ARMY OF OZ! THE SCARECROW TOLD ME YOU'D COME!

WHERE IS THE SCARECROW? I MUST FIND HIM!

HMM... THAT DOOR IS THE ONLY WAY OUT! WE CAN TAKE A NAP!

IF THEY TRY TO GET BY US, WE'LL WAKE UP!

I CAN'T TELL YOU MUCH, MISS GALE! WHEN EVERYTHING STARTED TO TURN TO STONE, THE SCARECROW PUT ME HERE TO WAIT FOR YOU!

BUT YOU WEREN'T TURNED TO STONE! WHY NOT?

BECAUSE I'M NOT ALIVE — AND NEVER WILL BE, THANK GOODNESS!

NOW, WIND UP MY THINKING! I MUST PLAN OUR ESCAPE!

WIND! WIND!

ZZZZZ
ZZZZZ

SCREEEK!

ASLEEP ON THE JOB, ARE THEY? HAND ME YOUR LUNCHPAIL, MISS GALE!

SDENG!

SDONG!

STOP THEM!

AFTER THEM!

DON'T LET THEM GET AWAY!

NOW I THINK WE'D BETTER MAKE OUR ESCAPE!

OH, POOR TIK TOK! SURELY HE CAN'T SURVIVE THIS!

BUT...

YEOW!

TUMP!

CRACK!

YAAAH!

BANG!

THE ROYAL ARMY OF OZ DEMANDS THAT YOU SURRENDER!

WHY, YOU SCRAP-METAL KETTLE! I'LL...

I'LL HAVE YOU KNOW I'M MADE OF PURE COPPER, SIR!

NOW—TELL ME WHAT HAS HAPPENED TO THE SCARECROW AND THE EMERALD CITY!

SOON...

THE NOME KING IS RESPONSIBLE! HE TOOK ALL THE EMERALDS AND TURNED EVERYONE TO STONE!

OH, MY GOODNESS! BILLINA, LOOK THERE!

IT'S THE TIN MAN— HE'S BEEN TURNED TO STONE!

AND LOOK AT THE COWARDLY LION! OH, MY POOR FRIENDS!

WHAT ABOUT THE SCARECROW? WHERE IS HE?

I DON'T KNOW ANYTHING ABOUT HIM!

YOU'LL HAVE TO ASK PRINCESS MOMBI!

WHEN THE NOME KING CONQUERED OZ, HE MADE HER THE RULER! WE WHEELERS ARE HER ARMY!

THIS IS HER PALACE! IF SHE KNEW I HAD TALKED TO YOU, SHE'D KILL ME!

PLEASE LET ME GO! I'LL BEHAVE!

I PROMISE YOU! I WON'T GIVE YOU ANY MORE TROUBLE!

YOU KNOW, BILLINA, THIS PLACE LOOKS FAMILIAR!

NOT TO ME! I DON'T LIKE IT — NOT ONE LITTLE BIT!

WHY, THE DOOR IS UNLOCKED!

SQUAWK!

LISTEN! DO YOU HEAR THAT MUSIC?

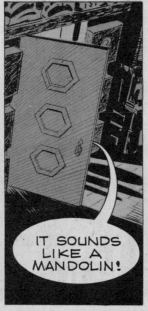

IT SOUNDS LIKE A MANDOLIN!

WE MUST BE CLOSE! IT'S GETTING LOUDER!

LOOK, TIK TOK!

HO-HUM!

PARDON ME, MA'AM — ARE YOU PRINCESS MOMBI?

YES, I AM! HELP ME UP!

COME WITH ME! I'M GOING TO PUT ON SOMETHING MORE APPROPRIATE!

BUT THE DRESS YOU'RE WEARING IS BEAUTIFUL!

WHO SAID ANYTHING ABOUT MY DRESS?

AH! NUMBER 4, I THINK!

BUT THOSE ARE ALL JUST... HEADS!

OF COURSE! YOU DON'T THINK I WEAR THIS OLD ONE ALL THE TIME, DO YOU?

AS I SAID— NUMBER 4! ISN'T SHE A PRETTY CHOICE?

SHE USUALLY WEARS ME TO MEET PEOPLE!

THERE! THAT'S BETTER! NOW— WHO MIGHT YOU BE?

HMMM...

I'M DOROTHY GALE, MA'AM— FROM KANSAS!

WELL... YOU WILL BE RATHER ATTRACTIVE ONE DAY! NOT BEAUTIFUL, YOU UNDER-STAND, BUT...

I DON'T CARE ABOUT THAT! I'VE COME TO ASK YOU...

KUT-KUT! OH, DEAR OLD KANSAS! IF ONLY...

MOM! IS THAT YOU?

WHO?

IT'S ME—JACK PUMPKIN-HEAD! YOUR SON!

BUT I DON'T HAVE A SON!

AWK! WHAT IS THIS FELLOW, WITH HIS GREAT ROUND HEAD—A MAN OR A MELON?

ARE YOU SURE YOU'RE NOT MY MOM? YOU LOOK A LOT LIKE HER!

I'M VERY SURE! WHO IS YOUR MOTHER?

SHE USED TO BE PRINCESS MOMBI'S SERVING MAID! BUT IT'S BEEN A LONG TIME SINCE I SAW HER!

ARE YOU QUITE SURE YOU'RE NOT HER?

YES, JACK! I'M SORRY!

WELL, THEN, DO YOU MIND IF I CALL YOU "MOM"? I'D LIKE THAT!

OF COURSE I DON'T MIND!

MY REAL MOM MADE ME TO FRIGHTEN MOMBI! IT WORKED, BUT MOMBI GOT ANGRY! SHE HAS QUITE A TEMPER!

YES, WE'VE SEEN THAT!

SHE LOCKED MY MOM AWAY, AND I HAVEN'T SEEN OR HEARD FROM HER SINCE!

AS FOR ME—MOMBI WAS GOING TO DESTROY ME, BUT SHE DECIDED TO USE ME TO TEST HER POWDER OF LIFE!

POWDER OF LIFE?

YES—IT'S ONE OF MOMBI'S MAGICS! SHE SPRINKLES IT ON SOMETHING AND SAYS, "WEAUGH! TEAUGH! PEAUGH!" THAT'S WHAT SHE DID TO ME!

AND HERE I AM—ALIVE!

KUT-KUT! DOES MOMBI HAVE ANY MORE OF THAT POWDER?

WELL, I'LL BE — A TALKING CHICKEN! WHAT WILL THEY THINK OF NEXT?

YES, MOMBI STILL HAS THE POWDER! SHE KEEPS IT IN CABINET 31! THE KEY HANGS FROM HER WRIST!

IF ONLY WE COULD GET HOLD OF THAT POWDER!

I'M SURE WE COULD USE IT TO ESCAPE, SO WE COULD HELP THE SCARECROW. BUT FIRST WE HAVE TO GET OUT OF HERE!

GET OUT OF HERE? WHY, NOTHING COULD BE EASIER, FOR ME, MOM!

*T*HAT NIGHT...

SSH...

QUIET!

KUT! KUT!

THAT WAS WONDERFUL, JACK PUMPKINHEAD! BUT WHY HAVEN'T YOU EVER TRIED TO ESCAPE BEFORE NOW?

WHY SHOULD I HAVE TRIED? I HAD NOWHERE TO ESCAPE TO!

UP IN THE TOWER...

WE MUST HURRY, TIKTOK! MOM IS COUNTING ON US!

BY ALL MEANS, JACK! LET US GATHER TOGETHER THE ARTICLES SHE SPECIFIED!

NOW, THE PALM LEAVES ARE TO BE TIED HERE, ALTHOUGH I HAVEN'T THE FAINTEST IDEA WHY!

AND THIS STUFFED GUMP'S HEAD IS TO BE AFFIXED TO THE FRONT!

MEANWHILE...

THERE'S MOMBI—AND SHE'S ASLEEP! I HOPE SHE...

...DOESN'T WAKE UP!

I GOT IT! NOW TO FIND CABINET NUMBER 31!

HERE IT IS — NUMBER 31!

CLICK!

THAT'S IT! THE POWDER OF LIFE!

POWDER OF LIFE

BAWK!

THIS FACE LOOKS FAMILIAR! I WONDER WHERE I'VE SEEN IT BEFORE!

THANK GOODNESS, BILLINA — WE GOT THE POWDER OF LIFE! LET'S GET BACK TO THE TOWER!

MY KEY! SOMEONE'S TAKEN MY KEY!

WHERE'S MY HEAD? I CAN'T SEE A THING WITHOUT MY HEAD!

WHEELERS! HELP ME! **STOP THEM!**

WEAUGH! TEAUGH!

PEAUGH!

GRASHHH

IT WORKED! WE'RE FLYING!

BA-A-WK!

MY CONGRATULATIONS, MISS GALE! YOUR PLAN WORKED!

EXCUSE ME— WILL SOMEONE PLEASE TELL ME WHAT'S GOING ON?

I DON'T KNOW IF THIS WAS SUCH A GOOD IDEA!

THERE I WAS QUIETLY MUNCHING GRASS, WHEN SUDDENLY EVERYTHING WENT BLACK!

NOW I HAVE A SOFA FOR A BODY, A BUNCH OF PEOPLE SITTING ON IT, AND PALM FRONDS FOR WINGS!

WINGS! BUT THAT MUST MEAN . . . OH, NO!

I'M FLYING! BUT GUMPS GALLOP—THEY CAN'T FLY!

HUSH, GUMP! WE FOUND YOU HANGING ON A WALL, STUFFED! BUT I SPRINKLED YOU WITH THE POWDER OF LIFE...

AND YOU CAME ALIVE! DO YOU KNOW WHERE THE NOME KING IS?

MY DEAR, GUMPS KNOW EVERYTHING! WE'RE HEADING RIGHT FOR HIS MOUNTAIN!

AWK! LOOK BELOW! OH, I WISH I WERE BACK IN KANSAS!

THE **WHEELERS!**

DON'T WORRY— THEY'RE GOING STRAIGHT TOWARD THE DEADLY DESERT!

IF THEY DON'T STOP, THEY'LL BE TURNED TO SAND!

WHOOPS!

WHOA!

OOH!

I'M GETTING TIRED, FOLKS! I THOUGHT WE WERE CLOSER TO THE MOUNTAIN!

GOLLY— WE CAN'T SEE ANYTHING IN THIS MIST!

OH, NO! WE'RE RIGHT ON TOP OF IT! **TURN!**

I DON'T THINK I CAN! HANG ON, EVERYONE!

WE'RE FALLING!

BAWK!

OHAHHHHHH!

THUMP

CRASH

I HOPE NO ONE ELSE WAS AROUND TO SEE THAT LANDING!

OOH! IT FEELS LIKE SOMETHING'S WRONG WITH MY HEAD!

BILLINA! WHERE IS BILLINA? AND WHY IS EVERYTHING UPSIDE-DOWN?

UP—DOWN, IT'S ALL THE SAME TO ME! WHO ARE YOU?

YOU'RE TRESSPASSING, YOU KNOW! THIS IS MY DOMAIN!

THAT IS THE NOME KING!

MY NAME IS DOROTHY GALE! I CAME TO RESCUE THE SCARE-CROW AND RESTORE THE EMERALD CITY!

NOT **THE** DOROTHY GALE — FROM KANSAS?

YES, YOUR MAJESTY! YOU MUST GIVE BACK THE EMERALDS YOU STOLE AND...

STOLE?!

NOW, WAIT ONE MINUTE, YOUNG LADY! I STOLE NOTHING! SINCE THEY CAME FROM MY MOUNTAIN, THOSE EMERALDS ARE **MINE**!

IT'S THE SCARECROW WHO WAS THE THIEF! THAT'S WHY I TOOK HIM PRISONER!

BUT THAT'S NOT FAIR — THE EMERALDS WERE ALREADY THERE WHEN HE BECAME KING!

COME, COME — TEARS FOR A MAN OF STRAW?

BUT HE'S MY FRIEND! I CAME TO RESCUE HIM — ALL THE WAY FROM KANSAS!

THERE, THERE, LITTLE DOROTHY! I WILL MAKE YOU A SPORTING PROPOSITION!

I LOVE ORNAMENTS, AND I DISPLAY THEM IN MY ORNAMENT ROOM!

MANY OF THESE ORNAMENTS USED TO BE MY ENEMIES, INCLUDING THE SCARECROW!

EACH OF YOU WILL GO INTO THE ROOM AND CHOOSE ONE ORNAMENT...

...THE ONE YOU THINK IS THE SCARECROW! YOU WILL TOUCH IT AND SAY, "OZ!" IF YOU ARE RIGHT, HE WILL BE RESTORED!

IF YOU ARE WRONG, YOU, TOO, WILL BECOME AN ORNAMENT!

NOW—WHO WANTS TO BE THE FIRST TO GUESS?

LET ME GO FIRST, MOM! IT'S NOT MUCH LOSS IF I AM WRONG!

THAT'S NOT TRUE, JACK, BUT SOMEONE MUST BE FIRST! GOOD LUCK!

HMMM...

HMM...

HM...

OZ!

POOOF!

TOO BAD, JACK—YOU MADE THE WRONG GUESS! NOW, WHO WILL BE NEXT?

BUT... BUT HE'S DISAPPEARED!

OF COURSE! HE'S NOW AN ORNAMENT! WELL, MAKE YOUR DECISION WHILE I TAKE CARE OF SOME-THING!

SO, MOMBI—I THOUGHT I TOLD YOU TO KEEP DOROTHY UNDER CONTROL! YET SHE ESCAPED YOU!

THAT WASN'T MY FAULT! SHE HAD HELP!

I CAME AS QUICKLY AS I COULD! I EVEN USED THE SECRET TUNNEL, SO I COULD WARN YOU!

SILENCE, WRETCH!

WELL, YOU'LL GET WHAT YOU DESERVE!

MAJESTY, LISTEN, I BEG YOU! DEAL WITH DOROTHY BEFORE SHE FINDS OUT ABOUT OZMA!

SHE IS VERY DANGEROUS, AND SHE EVEN HAS A CHICKEN WITH HER!

A CHICKEN?!

I SAW NO CHICKEN! IT MUST HAVE PERISHED WHEN THEY CRASHED ON MY MOUNTAIN! AND AS FOR DOROTHY— I HAVE MY WAYS!

MY WAY IS MUCH MORE AMUSING!

OZ!

POOF!

OH, DEAR— THEY ALL GUESSED WRONG— JACK, THE GUMP, AND NOW TIK TOK!

I DO WISH BILLINA WERE HERE TO HELP ME! ANYWAY, HERE GOES!

WHO WILL BE NEXT?

STAY A MOMENT, DOROTHY, DEAR! I HAVE ANOTHER PROPOSITION!

SCARECROW!

DOROTHY! I'M SO GLAD YOU GOT MY MESSAGE!

I'M HAPPIER STILL THAT YOU HAVE BEEN ABLE TO HELP ME!

MY GOODNESS... YOU WERE GREEN LIKE THE EMERALDS OF OZ...

QUICKLY! TOUCH EVERYTHING GREEN AND SAY "OZ!"

CONFOUND THE LUCK! SHE'S GUESSED THE SECRET! IF I DON'T STOP HER, SHE'LL DESTROY EVERY-THING!

OZ!

OZ!

OZ!

THIS CAN'T BE ALLOWED TO HAPPEN! NOMES! N-O-O-OMES!

DESTROY THEM! EXTERMINATE THEM!

OZ!

POOF!

MOM! IT'S YOU!

FIRE AND FLAMES! FUEL AND FURNACES! **THEY MUST DIE !!**

AWK! WHAT'S GOING ON HERE? WHERE AM I?

BILLINA!

I THOUGHT MY HEAD FELT A LITTLE STRANGE! THERE WAS A CHICKEN IN IT!

I FINALLY LAID MY EGG, AND WANTED A NAP, AND THIS LOOKED LIKE A GOOD PLACE!

LAID AN EGG?! IN MY DOMAIN? BUT EGGS ARE POISON TO NOMES!

SOON...

DOROTHY!

TIN WOODMAN! OH, HOW GLAD I AM TO SEE YOU!

AND LION! I WAS AFRAID I'D NEVER SEE YOU AGAIN!

AWK! DOROTHY, PLEASE INTRODUCE US! I'M THE ONE WHO LAID THE EGG, AFTER ALL!

SILENCE, EVERYONE, PLEASE!

I THINK THANKS ARE IN ORDER FOR OUR BRAVE RESCUERS!

TIK TOK, JACK PUMPKINHEAD, THE GUMP, BILLINA. AND...

...ABOVE ALL, THANKS TO DOROTHY, WHO CAME ALL THIS WAY TO HELP HER FRIENDS FROM OZ!

I KNOW WE ALL WISH DOROTHY COULD STAY WITH US FOREVER, BUT THERE ARE PEOPLE BACK IN KANSAS WHO MISS HER!

IN ANY CASE, SHE CAN RETURN WHENEVER SHE WISHES!

I THINK I WOULD RATHER STAY HERE!

AWK! ME, TOO, GUMP! A CHICKEN'S LIFE IN KANSAS IS SO BORING!

AND NOW I MUST MAKE AN ANNOUNCEMENT! I LEARNED FROM THE NOME KING THAT THERE IS AN HEIR TO THE THRONE OF OZ!

SHE IS PRINCESS OZMA! THE WITCH MOMBI HAD MADE HER A SLAVE!

LOOK, TIK TOK! THERE'S MOMBI, BUT SHE LOOKS ODD!

WHEN THE NOME KING'S MOUNTAIN FELL, SHE WAS SAVED, BUT HER MIND IS GONE!

I AM GLAD I FOUND OUT ABOUT OZMA, BECAUSE, YOU SEE...

...THIS CROWN IS MUCH TOO HEAVY FOR MY HEAD!

THAT'S ALL WELL AND GOOD, SCARECROW, BUT WHERE IS OZMA?

DOROTHY! COME HERE!

WHAT?

WHY, THERE'S SOMEONE THERE, BUT THERE ISN'T! IT'S A MIRROR!